Greater Than a Tourist Book Series

Reviews fr

CW01499837

I think the series is wonderfu
get information before visitin
-Seckin Zumbul, Izmir Turke

I am a world traveler who has read many trip guides but this one really made a difference for me. I would call it a heartfelt creation of a local guide expert instead of just a guide.

-Susy, Isla Holbox, Mexico

New to the area like me, this is a must have!

-Joe, Bloomington, USA

This is a good series that gets down to it when looking for things to do at your destination without having to read a novel for just a few ideas.

-Rachel, Monterey, USA

Good information to have to plan my trip to this destination.

-Pennie Farrell, Mexico

Great ideas for a port day.

-Mary Martin USA

Jamilah Beatrice

Aptly titled, you won't just be a tourist after reading this book. You'll be greater than a tourist!

-Alan Warner, Grand Rapids, USA

Thank you for a fantastic book.

-Don, Philadelphia, USA

Even though I only have three days to spend in San Miguel in an upcoming visit, I will use the author's suggestions to guide some of my time there. An easy read - with chapters named to guide me in directions I want to go.

-Robert Catapano, USA

Great insights from a local perspective! Useful information and a very good value!

-Sarah, USA

This series provides an in-depth experience through the eyes of a local. Reading these series will help you to travel the city in with confidence and it'll make your journey a unique one.

-Andrew Teoh, Ipoh, Malaysia

GREATER THAN A TOURIST – TRINIDAD & TOBAGO

50 Travel Tips from a Local

Jamilah Beatrice

Jamilah Beatrice

Cover designed by:
Cover Image: By cheesy42 [CC BY 2.0
(https://creativecommons.org/licenses/by/2.0)], via Wikimedia Commons

Edited by:

Greater Than a Tourist
Visit our website at www.GreaterThanaTourist.com

Lock Haven, PA
All rights reserved.
ISBN: 9781980921295

>TOURIST

50 TRAVEL TIPS FROM A LOCAL

Jamilah Beatrice

BOOK DESCRIPTION

Are you excited about planning your next trip?

Do you want to try something new?

Would you like some guidance from a local?

If you answered yes to any of these questions, then this Greater Than a Tourist book is for you.

Greater Than a Tourist- Greater Than a Tourist- Trinidad & Tobago   by Jamilah Beatrice offers the inside scoop on Trinidad & Tobago . Most travel books tell you how to travel like a tourist. Although there is nothing wrong with that, as part of the Greater Than a Tourist series, this book will give you travel tips from someone who has lived at your next travel destination.

In these pages, you will discover advice that will help you throughout your stay. This book will not tell you exact addresses or store hours but instead will give you excitement and knowledge from a local that you may not find in other smaller print travel books.

Travel like a local. Slow down, stay in one place, and get to know the people and the culture. By the time you finish this book, you will be eager and prepared to travel to your next destination.

Jamilah Beatrice

TABLE OF CONTENTS

15. Get Your Bitters- Angostura Distillery Tour
16. Make A River Lime, Caura River
17. Dinner And A Movie- One Woodbrook Place
18. Early Is Best, Maracas Waterfalls.
19. Tour The Emperor Valley Zoo
20. Watch The Turtles Come In, Grande Riviere
21. Dancing With Birds, Asa Wright Nature Centre
22. Spend The Day At Store Bay
23. Fall in Love at Acono Falls
24. D' Roti Shop, Recharge Here
25. Breathe Easy At Valencia Eco Resort
26. Experience Heaven On Earth At La Vega Estate
27. India In The Caribbean
28. See A Performance At NAPA
29. Shop away at the UPMarket
30. Go Green, Santa Cruz Green Market
31. Come Home To Entertainment And Cultural Savvy- Kaiso Blues Café
32. Dine-In At Gemstone Cineplex
33. Wine and Dine-In, Kariwak Village Holistic Haven And Hotel Restaurant, Tobago
34. Win Big On A Small Hike-Argyle Falls, Tobago
35. Own It At No Man's Land, Tobago
36. Quick Stop At Fort Milford, Tobago
37. Beginners Scuba Dive In, Tobago
38. Saturdays at Trincity Mall

DEDICATION

This book is dedicated to Julia.

Jamilah Beatrice

ABOUT THE AUTHOR

Jamilah is a bilingual outgoing advocate of cats and Korean dramas who currently comes from the city of San Juan. She loves quality time spent with her family on walks, ad hoc trips to here and there…everywhere. Her love for *tomatoes choka* at breakfast and *callalloo* at lunch is what undeniably makes her a *Trini*…

Jamilah Beatrice

HOW TO USE THIS BOOK

The Greater Than a Tourist book series was written by someone who has lived in an area for over three months. The goal of this book is to help travelers either dream or experience different locations by providing opinions from a local. The author has made suggestions based on their own experiences. Please do your own research before traveling to the area in case the suggested places are unavailable.

Jamilah Beatrice

FROM THE PUBLISHER

Traveling can be one of the most important parts of a person's life. The anticipation and memories that you have are some of the best. As a publisher of the Greater Than a Tourist book series, as well as the popular 50 Things to Know book series, we strive to help you learn about new places, spark your imagination, and inspire you. Wherever you are and whatever you do I wish you safe, fun, and inspiring travel.

Lisa Rusczyk Ed. D.
CZYK Publishing

Jamilah Beatrice

OUR STORY

Traveling is a passion of the "Greater than a Tourist" series creator. Lisa studied abroad in college, and for their honeymoon Lisa and her husband toured Europe. During her travels to Malta, an older man tried to give her some advice based on his own experience living on the island since he was a young boy. She was not sure if she should talk to the stranger but was interested in his advice. When traveling to some places she was wary to talk to locals because she was afraid that they weren't being genuine. Through her travels, Lisa learned how much locals had to share with tourists. Lisa created the "Greater Than a Tourist" book series to help connect people with locals. A topic that locals are very passionate about sharing.

Jamilah Beatrice

WELCOME TO
> TOURIST

Jamilah Beatrice

INTRODUCTION

"I haven't been everywhere, but it's on my list."
– Susan Sontag

A visit to my little twin island warrants a hefty Trini pat on the shoulder for a job well done on exploring this side of the Caribbean. With a modest population of only 1.372 million, you have struck a goldmine of cultural diversity immediately seen in the architecture, food and music. Moreover, the ins and outs of Trinidad and Tobago's natural, beautiful landscape will satisfy the appetite of the pickiest of enthusiasts; truly a paradise to discover.

Jamilah Beatrice

1. LEAVE YOUR WORRIES BEHIND, KNOCK ABOUT TOWN

The island like no other exudes a sense of relaxation which will calm your every travel anxiety. Trinbagonians (a blend of the words, Trinidadians and Tobagonians) are proud of their spicy food but more than that they take pride in connecting with and assisting others; especially newcomers to the island. Do not be surprised if you find yourself audience to a Trini who wanted tell you about all the friends they made while they were in some foreign country. So be at ease and chat away as if it were to an old friend. If lost, ask a cheerful pie man, fruit vendor or store clerk for assistance if needed. I thoroughly enjoy an active day of knocking about the cities of San Fernando, Princess Town and Port of Spain. There is always an interesting find or fun encounter to discover. So pick your town; rest assured a good samaritan will steer you on your way. Be prepared though, our finger pointing methods of providing directions could confuse the most attentive of folks. It's funny. Temperatures are high here so ensure to take along a litre of my favourite local Blue Waters to refresh your mind after a series of wrong turns. Most importantly, enjoy it; even the locals stray off the beaten path from time to time.

2. "KNOW" THE COUNTRY LIKE A LOCAL WITH PTSC

We get it! Our heat can sometimes be scorching and despite being the great adventurer you are within, this time you may opt for the back seat. With sightseers like you in mind the Public Transportation Service of Trinidad and Tobago (PTSC) has masterminded sightseeing through its "Know Your Country" tours. You get to cheaply travel in a spacious and comfy air-conditioned bus with the locals to some of the more famous natural sights on the island; even island hopping is offered. While in the city of Port of Spain I encourage you to visit the PTSC information desk at City Gate for a listing of upcoming tours. My all-time favourites are the Island Hopping tour and Port of Spain to Mayaro tour. Book one, pack a picnic basket, hop on board and get to "know" this country in pure PTSC comfort.

3. FOODIES TREAT YOURSELF TO LOCAL EATS

Embrace the opportunity to circle the world's largest roundabout, The Queen's Park Savannah. A local will direct you to the taxi stand if you ask. Be in awe as you encircle this giant but don't pass the foodie hub. After sundown the place is guaranteed to be buzzing with activity. Long lines interweave as patrons gather to sample local delicacies like phulorie, cow heel soup, cane juice, coconut water and sour-sop punch as well as a local take on foreign eats like beef burgers and buffalo wings. There's something for everyone. Bring the kids too.

4. PLAN A NIGHT OUT AT THE QUEEN'S

I'm sure you remember the Queen's Park Savannah in tip four. Well around you go again but this time your destination is the Queen's Hall. Revere in celebrating our local talent with us by calling or visiting the Hall's website to book your spot. Awaiting you is a host of budget friendly opportunities to behold our local talent: internationally renowned poets and comedians, soca artistes, child orchestras and many more.

5. LIME LIKE A TRINI ON D'AVENUE

You may or may not have heard of the term "liming;" a simple habit of relaxing and having fun with friends that Trinbagonians have put into overdrive. In short, we love to lime and strongly encourage you to do the same while with us. After all, you are on vacation. Ariapita Avenue is Port of Spain's more upscale liming spot of choice as it boasts over fifty stops (a few small-scale casinos included) at which you can grab the best eats and drinks, dance away and you guessed it…lime the night away too. The Avenue is a local Pangea with its wide offering of international cuisine, savoury creole bites, spicy street food and an array of cocktails served at several locations. Ladies feel free to don those fancy heels; gents, some chinos with dressy shoes will guarantee your entry into the more upscale pubs and clubs.

6. DETOX AT THE LA BREA PITCH LAKE SITE

If you have an appreciation for natural phenomena then this is the one for you. This giant of a world wonder is much like a living organism; picture the warm and wrinkled, surface of a rhino's back, stretching for acres upon acres each way. Walking along this cracked, uneven surface is in itself interesting, more so, when you dip into the therapeutic waters…you will not want to leave. Imagine relaxing in the steamy sulphur pools which enhance the awesomeness of this landmass. On arrival ensure to book a tour with an official tour guide to capitalize on getting your money's worth of information and time at the location. Wear sturdy shoes that can get wet and do bring a swim suit.

7. GOOD TO HIKE, THREE POOLS

You need only three reasons to trek through Trinidad's Northern Range. Demanding short bursts of energy at the right time, this journey on an upward spiralling path set in a backdrop of greenery and waist deep waters can prove to be a good workout and a countdown to the next event as each phase becomes more challenging. Prepare to break a nail or two ladies. Expect to relax on arrival at the highest and largest pool which sits at the base of a modest waterfall. Engage your inner daredevil to take the twenty foot plunge. Yes, the plunge! Eat well before this trip and take along a couple protein bars; fresh crisp and cool water is provided compliments of Mother Nature herself.

8. TRAVEL TO MARACAS BAY

This one is interesting and will most definitely appeal to the DIY crowd. I strongly recommend making this trip during the week as the weekend brings the entire population to Maracas. Two ways to get there: the very early air-conditioned PTSC bus service or the private minibuses at the corner of Prince and George St. Both are quite cheap and definitely trump hiring a taxi. The drive on the north coast road is roughly forty-five minutes each way. Do confirm the bus schedule at the service centre so you can catch the bus on the way back. If you miss it you can wait up to thirty minutes for a minibus back to Port-of-Spain. The beach facilities are currently being upgraded with stores and other tourist focused fittings which so far promise to enhance the experience. Facilities or not the bay's natural beauty and relaxing vibe is all you will need to enjoy this experience. Oh, that and our local "bake and shark" which you must try.

9. EXPERIENCE OUR SCIENCE CULTURE

The National Science Centre is an awesome place to visit, open Monday to Friday and a short drive from the Piarco International Airport. Adults may develop a newfound appreciation for the science in everyday living and kids can foster their creative genius here. Plus, it's a magnificent experience for a very affordable price, quoted in TTD. With approximately two hundred interactive exhibits both adults and children can enjoy activities centred on disaster awareness, animation, creativity and innovation, energy and the environment, the human body, sports and wellness, physical disabilities, and robotics. It will leave quite the impression.

10. RELIGIOUS DAY

Some activities are just too holy to ignore, even on vacation. Trinidad and Tobago is well known for its largely heterogeneous origins, the effect of which remains quite evident to date, particularly from a multi- religious standpoint. Embrace the dotting of various worship centres all within a small radius at any city hub; from the warm and many kingdom halls of Jehovah's Witnesses to the wide open Shiv Mandir in El Dorado. Several city hubs boast the chorus of Shango Baptists in March bedecked in white as they serenade passers-by on the pavements and the mosques of several suburban areas may mesmerize you, as was I, by the sound of the Islamic adzhan (call to prayer/worship) piercing the early morning. Like its countrymen Trinbagonians worship centres love to welcome visitors so just in case you feel compelled to visit, take along a shirt and don't be shy. Cheers to life on the island.

11. GO DOWN D' ISLANDS– GASPAR GRANDE

On this twelve kilometre long limestone rock you are in the Bocas del Dragón or dragon's mouth, and Venezuela's north-east coast lies just eleven more kilometres away. This day long tour affords you the luxury of capturing the rich history of the island and three points of interest you are most likely to visit. You will sail on over to the island and dock in at Point Baliene, a former whaling station. Apart from being an attraction in itself, it is a main drop off point for visitors to the Gasparee Caves which is the very highlight of this trip. Remember that not too interesting geography lesson on stalagmites and stalactites? The Gasparee Caves on Gaspar Grande are lined with them but these promise to reignite your interest as you feast your eyes on the cornucopia of colours, shapes and the soft glow of natural lighting that beautifies this space. To enter you must descend into the cavern which in itself creates a sensation of

23

entering a new world. You are encouraged to seek out the curious formations created by the crystals, among them a dinosaur head and two lovers hugging. However, the real star is the cave's translucent blue pond of about twenty feet deep. Engineered by the seeping in of underground seawater it is a sight to behold as the natural light filtering through depicts an azure blue and a sensation of looking up at a perfectly clear sky on a sunny day. On exiting the caves, depending on the weather you may be invited to bathe or picnic out at Bombshell Bay until sunset. What a day! You will have a sound night's sleep.

12. BAMBOO CATHEDRAL

If you are the active type and staying in the vicinity of Port of Spain or Chaguaramas then you can easily get to this location and capitalize on the terrain for early morning exercise and/or relaxation. Nevertheless all are welcome, this is a completely free activity and a tour guide is not required. The track starts off the Macqueripe Road just before Macqueripe Bay and is bordered by an awesome convergence of bamboo on each side arching gently into each other, hence the name. At the entrance do look on for the howler monkeys grooming themselves on the bamboo tops; it's a sight for sore eyes. This upward climb can become arduous but the furtive efforts of other enthusiasts will inspire you to keep up as you make your way to the remains of the World War II Tracking Station on the summit. Like a true gem this area has, for more than one hundred and fifty years, remained untouched.

13. TAKE THE PLUNGE, GUANAPO GORGES

For me this journey was all about the ten foot plunge on the way back down the river. It's been years and I still cherish it.One may opt to take the arduous land journey back but you would have been there and done that. No fun. Instead get soaked in the cool spring fresh currents and flow with the river between the mossy green gorges and become mystified by the canopies of trees that loom overhead. Mother Nature certainly spent an extra minute on this path. This scenic adventure is Discovery Channel worthy. Call the tour group to secure your spot and indicate if transportation must be arranged for you. This is usually a small fee plus the cost of the hike. Your tour company will meet up at the city of Arima, most likely, and from there you will proceed northeast towards the Heights of Aripo. The drive itself is uneventful but when you arrive0 at the hiking point, boy are you in for a treat. Note that safety equipment such as ropes and life vests are provided by the sufficiently staffed tour group. Take along a protein bar or two, some tour companies provide refreshments and wear good hiking shoes for this one.

14. BAT CAVE- GUANAPO

Dark, cramped, earthy and eerie is the only way to describe the interior of this modest once active dugout. Claustrophobes keep out but before even reaching the mouth of the cave you must put on the persona of a mountain goat to confidently make your way up. This steep incline calls out to your inner Tarzan as you are urged to define your own path while grabbing firmly onto tree trunks, jutting rocks and hanging vines. The journey up, some may say, is more intriguing than the cave itself. For safety, wear sturdy shoes with good grips.

15. GET YOUR BITTERS- ANGOSTURA DISTILLERY TOUR

Angostura Bitters- a household name in Trinidad and Tobago and the final ingredient to multiple local beverages enjoyed every day. Whether you are flavouring a hot cup of milk tea in the morning, mixing up a beastly cold glass of home-style mauby or topping off a glass of Angostura rum on the rocks, this staple makes it all go down refreshingly smooth. You are sure to spot it in the local bars but if you don't, then leave the bar. Leave the bar and book your Angostura Distillery bi-weekly tour which is available to the general public. The facility boasts its own museum and art gallery, auditorium and hospitality suites for visitor tours. A former World Spirits awardee, the Angostura Distillery will impress you with its rich history brewed into superior world renowned products. Be sure to pick up a bottle of bitters from the on-site retail store, it would make an ideal gift.

16. MAKE A RIVER LIME, CAURA RIVER

In Trinidad and Tobago, a river lime is a customary event and a much anticipated way to celebrate a long weekend or holiday. With family and/or friends, a pot of pelau or curry goat and a wide array of drinks to take you much into the evening the Caura Valley is the number one spot for a river lime. It lies north of Trinidad's East-West corridor and if you are attentive enough you may be guided to the location by the loud blast of East Indian tassa music, a clear sign of an on-going river lime up ahead. The river is very popular due to the moderate flow of crisp clear water and natural vegetation which shrouds the area yet offers a few clearings perfect for on-site cooking. This high popularity can be somewhat of a double edged sword on the weekends as community residents and non-residents alike flock to this star location. The most coveted spots though are the two pools at the site of the abandoned pump house. A few Amerindian styled shelters have been erected to accentuate the experience on the river and can provide additional shelter from the sunlight which pushes through the trees but generally this area is well shaded. As you may want to take along a half-days' worth of supplies, I recommend renting a vehicle for the day or organizing private transportation for drop off and pick up.

17. DINNER AND A MOVIE- ONE WOODBROOK PLACE

Considering a movie night? With only two main social hubs in the Port of Spain area for this activity this chic hotspot exudes an air of elegance and will add a touch of old world class to your date night. This compound is home to a few upscale restaurants which are growing in popularity as Trinidad's wine culture expands. Furthermore mix and blend of European and Mediterranean cuisine offered here will surely delight your taste buds. A few of the cafes provide an opportunity to dine on the veranda while enjoying the evening sky and city lights. To compliment this fine dining experience, you must stroll on over to the Digicel IMAX cinema. It is very easy to differentiate the superior viewing experience you are guaranteed here from the rest. Truly enjoy your viewing experience with a larger screen, enhanced picture quality and you may even opt to purchase VIP tickets and relax into the plush leather seating with the best view the room can offer. An honourable mention is the opportunity albeit pricey there is an opportunity to rent a unit per night but this should be arranged beforehand as these units are usually the preferred locale for expats.

18. EARLY IS BEST, MARACAS WATERFALLS.

This is a journey that requires little effort yet you can reap great rewards from the island's highest waterfall- to bathe there is invigorating. The easy accessibility is what makes this trip most appealing as a tour guide is not necessary. Nestled in the Maracas Valley, Waterfall Road is pretty self-explanatory. For this journey you are advised to rise before the chickens in order to capitalize on the cool clean crisp air that will ease your way as you ascend this delicate path. This woodsy locale also gets dark well before sundown so your preparedness to leave early is a must. Although the fall is more majestic during the rainy season be extra careful as some areas may become quite slippery. There is a small picnic area at the site and a pool on the way up which is ideal for swimming. I highly recommend taking a camera to capture the spectacular views that await you.

19. TOUR THE EMPEROR VALLEY ZOO

Enjoy the antics of the red howlers or play a game of spot the green iguanas with the kids. There are so many more local creatures to meet here. A visit to a foreign zoo is essentially the silent goal of many animal enthusiasts. This one is a double delight as the Botanical Gardens are but a stone's throw away, free of charge and offer an opportunity to relax among the most sacred of Trinidad's flora after a fun filled day at the zoo. Named after our very own Emperor butterfly, the Emperor Valley Zoo exists to educate the population on the animal kingdom while continuously seeking to enhance the lives of its captive animals. The information plate posted at every display truly will enhance your understanding of the creation before you and I hope you also develop an appreciation for the islands local fauna and flora on which much emphasis is placed as evidenced in the construct which allows as up-close of a view as is safely possible. Although the zoo showcases some exotic species, the majority are uniquely from Trinidad and Tobago and the adjacent South American continent. A mid-morning weekday visit is recommended to avoid the crowds and get your fair share of the sights. A street-food café and ice-cream parlour are located on site so light lunch and dessert are covered on this perfect locale for a family outing.

20. WATCH THE TURTLES COME IN, GRANDE RIVIERE

There are not many places where one can experience this iconic moment in the lives on an endangered species. Trinidad and Tobago is one of the few places in the world lucky enough to continue to host these sea mammoths that populate our shores each year. While some visitors plan their vacation around this event others relish in the perfect coincidence and walk away with a lifelong appreciation for the experience. Nevertheless, from March to August each month brings its wonders. As far as you can see under the moonlit sky thousands of turtles will suddenly appear from the ocean to dot the sandy shores. To safeguard the process onlookers are required to use infrared lighting only. This tour operated experience lasts the entire night so you are most likely to observe a laying close up, well worth it. From June to August thousands of hatchlings climb out from their nests and make their way to sea, guaranteed to return to this very shore on which they were born, just like their predecessors. Dress warmly to protect against the chilly sea breeze and sand flies. I recommend a hoodie. Most importantly speak in hushed tones so as not to discourage the sea turtles. We wish to welcome them for many more years to come. You too may want to share this experience with your grandchildren one day.

21. DANCING WITH BIRDS, ASA WRIGHT NATURE CENTRE

To be in the presence of this colourful sight is inspiring enough to make you want to dance away. Indeed, one of the smallest extant bird species dwells right here in Trinidad and Tobago and thrives in droves at the Asa Wright Nature Centre, a conservation for these little gifts of nature and many more wildlife species. This reserve receives its annual share of bird watchers from around the world and is known by local wildlife enthusiasts as the very place to comfortably experience the nocturnal activities of the valley. Yes, guest rooms are available on site but prepare to make a booking well in advance of your arrival. You will appreciate the daily tours led by friendly and extremely informative guides who are happy to share their first-hand knowledge of the Centre and its treasures. While sitting on the veranda where multiple birdfeeders attract these helicopter-like avian damsels, I loved watching and hearing them whizz by, only to suddenly stop mid-flight to show off their amazing beauty. What a delight! Finally, spare some time to seek out the perfectly chilled spring water that trickles into a tiny, tiny pool just outside of the Centre. It will invigorate and nourish your very soul.

22. SPEND THE DAY AT STORE BAY

This one takes you to the very beautiful serene island of Tobago. So, you have just arrived and already there is much to do. I thoroughly enjoyed my weekend trips to Store Bay and all that it had to offer. This bay is always perfect for swimming; even the shyest of swimmers will be soothed by the calm ebb and flow of the blue waters here. Located a stone's throw away from the ANR Robinson International Airport you can hop off the plane and be in the water in a matter of minutes; four minutes to be exact, via Store Bay Connector Road. Fathom touching the ocean floor? Discover what wonders lie out there when you take the tour of the Buccoo Reef on the glass bottom boat. You can get your tickets right at Store Bay. Hunger is not an issue at Store Bay as a wide variety of local and authentically Tobagonian cuisine is served within the vicinity. Options include the fanciful dishes served up at the nearby hotels or the fanciful and cheap home-style cuisine served up at multiple outlets around the area and on the beach itself. Nothing, nothing says Store Bay like a bag of spicy pommecythere chow (pronounced [pommeseetay]) and a beastly cold Carib beer. Enjoy!

23. FALL IN LOVE AT ACONO FALLS

Do you believe that adventure can make the heart flutter? Well this forty minute journey to the Acono Falls is sure to set your atria into full gear. Furthermore, the natural and mystical beauty you will encounter along the way will ignite your senses and bring out your inner photographer; but be mindful to save some storage space for the main event, a phenomenal sight to behold. The fun begins at an inactive road formerly used by a cocoa estate, now abandoned. Prepare to get wet as you veer off trail into the river that flows through the Maracas Valley. Ensure to have a solid meal beforehand as you will need your strength; this is an upward trek through a river with much variation in its makeup before arriving at the site of the main event. Acono Falls cascades gracefully into a plunge pool which remains placid enough for light swimming. Wear your swimsuit under your hiking clothes otherwise the changing facilities available would be the trunks of trees and spread of bushes. The water is refreshingly very crisp and is sure to encourage some cuddling.

24. D' ROTI SHOP, RECHARGE HERE

Lunchtime! The streets and avenues of Trinidad are flooded with the hungry busybodies eagerly making their way to my favourite roti hub, located in San Juan. You can follow them onto Back Chain Street just off El Socorro Road and pop into any one of these three extremely packed roti shops located either opposite or adjacent to each other. I think of them as the three musketeers of the curry world, each with its own pizazz but all equally skilled in their art. Be prepared to stand in a long snaking line; I promise it will be worth your while. This sort of eatery is usually abuzz with activity so pay attention as your chance to place your order at the cashier's counter nears. Ensure to speak up amidst the chorus of murmurs as folks select their desired sides. Whether it's at Patraj, Sylvies or Ali's you will emerge a victor. The main stays are soft and flavour packed dhalphurie or paratha rotis with a choice of meat (typical options are curried chicken, beef, goat or shrimp) and sides of savoury potato (aloo) and chickpeas (channa), pumpkin, bhaji (spinach) and others. I recommend a dhalphurie wrap for easier consumption and please ensure to indicate whether or not you want pepper sauce. Trinidadian hot sauce is very spicy and very delicious. Most Trinidadians will furtively nod in agreement when I suggest an accompanying beverage of either Coca Cola or a "red Solo" to perfect this meal.

25. BREATHE EASY AT VALENCIA ECO RESORT

Do you fancy the great outdoors? At the foothills of Trinidad's Northern Range rests a ten-acre spread of polished greenery called the Valencia Eco Resort. Let the thrill of disembarking a plane and bustling off to a busy city hotel wear off; instead, relax into nature's luxury that this eco haven has to offer. Enjoy the best of both worlds as the facility offers overnight air-conditioned cabana-styled accommodation that matches the comfort of city hotels and exceeds expectations through its broad spectrum of activities to keep you thoroughly entertained. Picture perfect is the scenery of over one thousand uniquely Caribbean fruit trees which attract a myriad of wildlife, including birds and butterflies...and you can freely walk amongst such beauty. Furthermore, with tens of sporting options, from fishing to archery, you simply can never be bored. Animal lovers are encouraged to enjoy the special facility much akin to a miniature petting zoo where one can interact with the local fauna. Plan a family day and have fun with outdoor cooking under one of the many carrat sheds provided for your use. Whatever brings you to this lovely twin island, rest assured that the deep relaxation guaranteed at the Valencia Eco Resort will ensure your return year after year, after year.

26. EXPERIENCE HEAVEN ON EARTH AT LA VEGA ESTATE

To be surrounded by natural beauty is an elusive goal of many in these modern times. To be enthralled by the overarching sense of peace exuded by this natural landscape will be an experience of a lifetime which you can share with your loved ones. Like a Trini you too can experience it all at La Vega: acres upon acres of lush greenery, a hideaway so perfect for a day of bonding with loved ones. Furthermore, the estate is open to your planned events from weddings to corporate workshops, anything really. Special spots like the Garden of Meditation and Bamboo Nursery present the ideal environment for a stroll, just perfect for newlyweds. Guided tours of the estate's green houses, orchards and fields will have you excited to explore the tastes and textures of our local cuisine. Whether bird watching, fishing, hiking or swimming, you are sure to find an activity to match your recreational goals.

27. INDIA IN THE CARIBBEAN

Well worth the trip to central Trinidad, you will be privy to sights which offer a sample of India, right here in the Caribbean, at a fraction of the cost, considering the airfare of course. The much heralded Hanuman Murti which rests majestically in the atrium of Carapichaima and ascends into the sky for a stunning eighty-five feet reportedly makes it the largest one of Hanuman outside of India and a popular religious site in Trinidad. What will make this site even more interesting to you is the subtle pink hued Dattareya Temple with bold eye-catching displays of Hindu deities from wall to ceiling. You may want to take a photo of the ceiling with you as a souvenir. Do not end this religious tour here; a seven-minute drive on via Orange Field Road is the fastest route to the Indian Caribbean Museum of Trinidad and Tobago where you will be immersed in a flood of Trinidad's East Indian heritage told through artefacts, preserved books and photographs. The museum leads you to the Hindu pilgrimage site, the Temple in the Sea.

28. SEE A PERFORMANCE AT NAPA

The National Academy for the Performing Arts (NAPA) is a majestic state-of the-art architectural masterpiece, the most attractive of the city's modern installations. You will want to bring your camera. Located at the heels of the world's largest roundabout, NAPA pays homage particularly to the island's rich steel pan culture and talent showcasing and is an ideal location to experience the higher cultural offerings of Trinidad and Tobago. Just like its unique architectural design, it is host to one of a kind cultural events, shows and performances which celebrate local and West Indian heritage, even placing a comedic spin on the dark times of our local history.

To truly experience the offerings of the local entertainment scene, make a booking at this location.

29. SHOP AWAY AT THE UPMARKET

If your stay on the island encompasses a weekend then consider yourself lucky to experience the convergence of totally local and handcrafted gems you will find at the Up Market. This event is held every month and tends to increase in frequency leading up to the Christmas holidays. You will delight in all this growing craft, food and small business market has to offer as it presents a great opportunity to take back a host of cool souvenirs which will always remind you of the good times spent here. The main location for this market is at the Woodbrook Youth Facility which is easily accessible via several taxi routes or the minibus from the city centre. Parking is widely available at the Stadium just next door. For most, what intrigues and encourages patrons to return is the trust built from one on one interactions with the dedicated and passionate entrepreneurs, crafters and chefs that are right there to

present their products. Total transparency is a high
selling point here, well worth the experience.

30. GO GREEN, SANTA CRUZ GREEN MARKET

Vacation time usually finds one up at the hour of
the rooster from sheer excitement alone. Why waste
an early morning simply being excited just to be here
when you can go places, go green, go early? I like to
go to the Santa Cruz Green Market on an empty
stomach just to break the fast with the one of a kind
cocoa tea brewed to sheer smooth perfection. Nothing
makes my Saturday better than this. Next up is the
thrill of being first in line at the local produce section
where I delight in choosing from the freshest of farm
goods. Mixology is evidently bountiful as patrons
flock the cosmetic sections for the offerings of
products, some organic, which have become so
essential to maintaining radiant skin under the
Caribbean sun; they are delectable too. By the way,
grab the opportunity to don a plethora of handcrafted
items; most sellers won't mind if you try on their
unique items if it helps you decide on the right one
for you. This close-knit community offers a friendly

and comfortable environment that will get you chatting in no time with sellers and patrons alike. You will leave with a light heart, a full stomach and, perhaps, an extended list of friends.

31. COME HOME TO ENTERTAINMENT AND CULTURAL SAVVY– KAISO BLUES CAFÉ

You will quickly understand that you have hit a cultural jackpot when you step into the Kaiso Blues Café. A cosy, intimate vibe akin to a grand bohemian get together mixed with the ambience of an artsy jazz club compels you to relax and unwind as you experience the true essence of the Caribbean. Phenomenal is the variety of entertainment offered at this location and outstanding is the quality of live and captivating performances that will woo you to return again and again, and again. Always abuzz with shows, live entertainment, music and dancing the host of this locale has succeeded greatly in creating an ideal oasis for the convergence of artistes and fans. You will enjoy the night whatever the performance. Service here is fit for a king as this quaint corner offers in-house cocktails with superior bar service and highly attentive and friendly staff. You must visit!

32. DINE-IN AT GEMSTONE CINEPLEX

The first of its kind in Trinidad and Tobago this dine-in cineplex is truly a unique take on the dinner and a movie experience. For avid movie goers who are just bored of the mundane and can forgo more than a few dollars for a five-star viewing/dining experience, I highly recommend this option. With luxurious plush leather seating in a classy uncluttered personalized space and full service in house restaurant you are sure to feel like a star. I strongly recommend taking along a sweater or scarf to keep warm as the indoor temperature can dip pretty low. Nevertheless, this upscale mini adventure in the city is sure to add a touch of class on any special evening out on the town in the city of Port of Spain.

33. WINE AND DINE-IN, KARIWAK VILLAGE HOLISTIC HAVEN AND HOTEL RESTAURANT, TOBAGO

Until you discover this one of a kind gem you will not believe that in walking distance, mere minutes away from the airport in Crown Point rests such an enchanted space, the Kariwak Village Hotel. Tucked away just off the Store Bay Branch Road, the soothing ambiance of this locale can melt away any tension. It is just the right stop for you after touchdown. I recommend a weekend booking to capitalize on dinner with live music for an unforgettable night of spot on entertainment and dancing. The food is always divine with lots of fresh vegetables and the fish is a must. You must not leave without trying a glass of their special rum punch. Breakfast and lunch is also available and presents the added bonus of touring the garden after which you may not want to leave. That said, and if you are lucky enough to secure a booking this is the perfect spot at which you can spend your last day in Tobago. With the advantage of being a stone's throw away from both beach and airport and having all meals offered in one location you can enjoy your stay to the fullest while thanking this godsend for a hassle-free departure back home.

34. WIN BIG ON A SMALL HIKE—ARGYLE FALLS, TOBAGO

The journey to this three-tiered cascade is fairly easy, fun and stimulating. You will begin in Roxborough on Tobago's north-east side and make your way to the Roxborough Visitor Service Office to pay the entrance fee. While a tour guide service may be provided one is not necessary for this clearly defined trail. Nevertheless, you should exercise some caution during the rainy season, as the rapid flows may prevent some from venturing on to the higher pools. So on immediate entrance you are greeted by the sounds and sights of birds, butterflies and yes, the falls. Fifteen minutes is all it takes to step into the crisp and chilly waters of the first pool which is just gorgeous but better lies ahead. Non-swimmers need not worry as the site is outfitted with ropes and flotation apparatus to ease you along. The pool at the top is the smallest but deepest and just right for swimming plunging and diving. A side adventure for some is the mini journey through the bushy side-path between pool one and two where you can shimmy your way up and into natural tubs formed by the eroded rock. The sensation of gushing water upon your back is far superior to a thirty-minute massage at any spa. Refreshing!

35. OWN IT AT NO MAN'S LAND, TOBAGO

Near the Bon Accord Lagoon, this uninhabited wetland, only accessible by sea is a pristine strip of paradise bound to make it on your personal list of best trips ever. Internationally protected under the Ramsar Convention, consider your fortune in being privy to the impenetrable mangroves of this beautiful coastal wetland and its surrounding area. Capitalize on this learning experience as you are completely free to walk about and explore to your heart's content. I recommend a full-service tour operator which will add a touch of magic to this experience by creating the best possible scenarios to suit your entertainment needs. My personal favourite tour company is Fish Tobago Tours because they consistently show off their expertise in customer care, even capturing the memories through photographing and video graphing your experiences so you can have all the uninterrupted fun. Moreover, you can look forward to scrumptious beach barbecues, traditional rum punch and a day, better yet a night, of dancing around a bonfire on this beautiful spit of white coral sand that breaks the kaleidoscope of the surrounding ocean.

36. QUICK STOP AT FORT MILFORD, TOBAGO

Before the Paris Treaty, this little island changed hands a whopping thirty-three times. The Brits won it over in the end and you can peek into this bit of history at little Fort Milford. After all, the history is in the ruins. The island is awash with forts but to me Fort Milford is special for its very close proximity (five minutes walking) to the airport, free entry and beautifully preserved lookout which doubles as a mini history lesson on Tobago's heritage; so worth the few minutes it takes to read the signs. What better place is there to wait out your departure from the island?

Relax under the shade provided by the low hanging trees and enjoy the views overlooking the bay but don't forget your flight; this spot is so serene you just might fall asleep.   Fort Milford provides an added bonus to anyone staying in nearby hotels such as the Karpiak Village; from there you could be before the best of views and the most beautiful of sunsets in mere minutes.

37. BEGINNERS SCUBA DIVE IN, TOBAGO

This is an ode to the first timers. As islanders we understand our great fortune in being surrounded by great bodies of water; tenfold is the fortune of being located in the Tropics. The aquatic life here is one of the best and most scenic in the world. You just have to dive in. Inexperience is no problem at all as Tobago is quite accommodating offering shallow-reef dives just perfect for beginners, especially around Speyside and Charlotteville located on the island's north side. The island itself is dotted with dive shops but those which are members of the Association of Tobago Dive Operators are the best and safest pick. A good experience for a first timer is at the Kariwak

Reef: typically flat with a depth of six metres, closed with no current. Tons of spectacular aquatic life will keep you interested in your new environment; try spotting the trumpet fish, they do a great job of imitating the coral.

38. SATURDAYS AT TRINCITY MALL

A fifteen minute drive from the airport will get you to this all in one shopping centre which is quite popular with the locals, especially on Saturdays. I have even seen some tourists make good use of the Port of Spain-Piarco route of the PTSC bus service which is a very affordable way to get around. However you choose to get there, you can have a full day of activities. Catch the latest movie with your group at the onsite theatre, Caribbean Cinemas Eight, eat nothing but popcorn drink nothing but water because just outside over twenty-five eateries, including a few upscale restaurants offering a wide array of local and international cuisine await your arrival. I think it is right to say that the options available perfectly reflect the multiethnic composition of the island; my all-time favourite is arabian food.

North-American fast food options are also available. Shopping is made super easy with a multitude of mini stores offering a host of goods from craft and local art to clothing and electronics. Feel free to stock up on supplies at one of the nation's leading supermakets located at the new wing of the mall; its inhouse bakery and cafe guarantees fresh bread daily and a warming cup of coffee. Did I mention the spa? Trincity Mall has a spa...and a hair salon. Ladies I've said enough.

39. VISIT A BIRDWATCHER'S PARADISE, ADEVENTURE FARM AND NATURE RESERVE, TOBAGO.

Allow me to clear this up before any misunderstandings arise. Neither is it a farm nor is it a nature park, however, it is a stunningly beautiful garden space with a few slightly hilly trails that provides the best bird watching experience ever. An hour or so is what it would take to peruse this slice of Eden but you are guaranteed to stay longer from sheer delight over the eye-catching views as the birds consistently come in to sample the fruits and seeds laid out by owners and staff. Imagine being a mere arm's length away from all six species of humming birds which hover boldly, in all their colourful splendour, before your eyes or witness the true highlight, the influx of several other species flocking to the feeders at the chime of a bell. The most knowledgeable of staff are there to guide you through should you require some information on what you see; the service is impeccable. I particularly like (so will you) that the smoothies available are made from the fruit of the trees (mango) at the location. The fresher the better! Also, while you sip on your beverage you can select a book or pamphlet and proceed to the seating area which is perfectly positioned for up close viewing of the wildlife that swoop down to sample the treats put out for them. Also, this vantage point presents a great photo opp. So make the trip to Plymouth and hop onto Arnos Vale Road which leads to this avian haven. You must not miss out.

40. BE ONE WITH THE HORSES, TOBAGO

Just how much will you like Being With Horses? Would you like a truly special two hour experience spending time with horses? Learn how to care for them, communicate with them and have tons of fun on horseback in the crystal waters of Bucco Bay. If you choose this activity you are guaranteed to have a magical day. Apart from doing something truly different in Tobago, you will gain a new appreciation for these gentle giants. Being With Horses is a group that handles their horses with love and great care which is seen in the easy-going personalities of each equestrian beauty during your riding experience. You will enjoy observing the behaviours of the horses as they, just as much as you do, enjoy the tour: through villages, on the seashore and through the waves (bring a change of clothes). Have fun picking your horse and please dress comfortably. Apart from a limit on persons over one hundred and ninety pounds, all are welcome and persons of all ages with no prior riding experience are very welcome to take this tour (yay). You will be glad to know that a resident photographer is available (yay) to capture those Kodak moments.

41. SEE SCARLET, CARONI SWAMP AND BIRD SANCTUARY

From October to March every year the evergreen trees of the Caroni Wetlands turn crimson. This is the magical sight of Trinidad's most spectacular national treasure, the Scarlet Ibis, flocking in from Venezuela to settle into their breeding grounds. These red long-legged beauties are extremely shy and take refuge in the internationally protected wetlands of Caroni, a Ramsar Site. As one of the island's most valued tourist attraction this boat tour down the picturesque Caroni channel to the main nesting area is extremely budget friendly (worth more than the cost) and typically lasts two hours. The boats leave at 4pm so be on-time. A more personalized experience with extended hours at the wetlands and the best seats on the boat is offered by some tour companies, but for me the standard tour is enough to keep the mystery alive. The journey itself is very scenic (mangroves on both sides) and informative which makes it great fun.

Jamilah Beatrice

I recommend boarding the boat first so you can access either the front or back of the boat which provides the best views. You will appreciate this spot as you enjoy your first-hand view of the birds coming in at sunset to colour the trees. From a distance you will see a host of other creatures: birds, crabs and coiled up boas but, of course, the star here is the Scarlet Ibis. Nature is all around so naturally you ought to take along a good bug repellent.

42. PLAY A ROUND OF GOLF, ST. ANDREWS GOLF CLUB

This is by far the best golf course in Trinidad and Tobago, a must-visit for established golfers and amateurs alike. I love being greeted with a beautiful bird's eye view of this eighteen-hole walking course which is well maintained and very posh. Snuggled away in the hills for a perfectly peaceful day, this facility sports its own restaurant, pool, sport shop and members club. The restaurant's menu options are fairly extensive, well priced and offer poolside cutters for guests who prefer to lounge in the shaded pool area instead of golfing. This facility is quite upscale

and exudes elegance; that said do refer to the website
for guidelines on their strict dress code in effect. This
is just the place to have fun with friends: after a game
the fully equipped bar is the best place to further
unwind with a glass of bourbon on the rocks. Much
akin to the pleasant and crisp environment, the staff
and caddies are a breath of fresh air: very professional
and welcoming, not to mention helpful.

43. ZIP THROUGH THE TREETOPS, MACQUERIPE BAY

Soar through the cool green treetops at Macqueripe
Bay, where this scenic adventure will begin. Some
tour groups offer hotel pickup which is useful to have
on the weekend when heading to this location. Ask
about this. You will be greatly entertained along the
seven-route course outfitted with net bridges to test
your nerves and canopy walks to wow your senses.
Heights of up to one hundred feet bestow the
unchallenged beauty of the bay below. You need not
make an appointment to enjoy this activity which is
offered Tuesday to Sunday from morning to late
afternoon. Just show up! It's quite affordable too and I

recommend cash payment. Just relax as you will be in the capable hands of trained personnel who will offer tips for a smooth sailing experience through the trees. How amazing is it that the facility caters for children as well (three to nine years old)? This trip is simply ideal for a fun filled family day out with the entire gang; with the beach just below and bike rental facilities nearby the opportunities are endless. I recommend a mid-morning start to capitalize on all of the awesome perks at this location.

44. PADDLE AWAY WITH STAND UP PADDLE, TOBAGO

Stand-up paddle boarding is a fun activity, an ancient tradition among fisher folk the world over. Participation in this activity requires an ability to balance over the ebb and flow of relatively calm waters and a sense of adventure. Is this you? The clear crisp waters off the island of Tobago makes this experience ten, no, a hundred times more enjoyable, not to mention the wide array of marine life to discover. Moreover, with great tips and tons of experience from the Staff at Stand Up Paddle Tobago, you will feel like an ancient warrior out on the hunt. Memories will last a lifetime. Visit Stand Up Paddle Tobago's website to see the list of tours offered to figure out what is best for you or your group. I strongly recommend taking the night-time bioluminescence tour; this is the stuff of Discovery Channel. This is a must, an experience of a lifetime. I dare say though, the regular route is not for the faint hearted or unfit as this journey covers roughly six kilometres so make sure you can swim and increase your endurance before embarking on this cool sporting journey. Even if you are not the stand-up paddle boarding type, fear not, kayaks are also an option and at least give you a great view of the fish. For the less experienced, a river tour is your best bet, still to be the highlight of your holiday.

45. FEAST! BLUE FOOD FESTIVAL, TOBAGO

As for me, the best form of Travel is experiential and this October fest is one you don't want to miss. Meet up with local Tobagonians and foreigners the world over to connect with Tobago's heritage through its sumptuous "blue food," mainly dasheen, which is the highlight of this event. Other root crops are showcased too. Indeed, the warm culture of Tobago is in its food. Thousands will flock to this annual festival just to sample the abundant culinary innovations and mingle with fellow foodies. The event usually runs from mid-morning to late evening and showcases a series of dishes concurrent with standard meal times. I don't mind planning my day's activities around this fete to capitalize on the breakfast, lunch, dinner...and dessert. Creations made from using the entire dasheen plant are indeed innovative: from cakes and cookies to wine and quiche. You name it! It's been made. Much apart from the attraction of mouth-watering signature delicacies is the allure of cultural interaction. You will feel one with the island's culture as guests are called to sample the creations of local chefs; even see first-hand how they prepare signature dishes at their open demonstrations. Revel in the local upbeat entertainment as sweet soca and calypso notes perfume the air. If you are looking for something truly culturally enriching, something which upholds Tobago heritage, this is the place to be.

46. PICK YOUR GOAT, BUCCOO GOAT RACE FESTIVAL

The Buccoo community keeps a stronghold on Tobago's heritage by the dedicated continuity of this pastime which is upwards of eighty years old. Why not? A great opportunity to share in the culture of Tobago is to go see this nationwide sport which attracts hundreds of families every year. This fun activity held at the Buccoo Stadium is a great way to kick it with the locals. Many open up their homes to spectators to offer home cooked dishes, so you need not ponder on what you will eat there, options are plentiful. Also, the streets are lined with booths offering trinkets, printed T-shirts and home style cooking to guests. More so, Easter Tuesday in Tobago has been officially dubbed "Goat Races Day," however crab racing at the same location goes hand in hand, so you will be doubly entertained. Believe me, it's a big deal! The races mimic traditional horse racing meets but pack a belly full of laughs, high levels of creativity and innovation, as you will see. Nevertheless, it is very structured with its own set of rules and classification for participants which highlights the seriousness applied to the sport and participants. Just perfect for tourists, you will be impressed by the lasting impression it leaves in your heart. As you continue your life's travels, you surely will never forget the goat races of little Tobago.

47. FUN IN JUNE, NATIONAL FRUIT FESTIVAL

Set in the month of June in south Trinidad this national festival is a superb way to emphasize the importance of plants, fruits and agriculture in our daily lives. This festival of fruits is both creative and educational. Although attention is cast on the local situation the concept can be applied to any environment and to anyone desirous of attaining healthy eating habits. If you have kids, this is a great event which will surely make a positive impact on their food preferences and encourage interest in your own country's forgotten foods, which are very healthy. Most impressive is the use of various fruit carved out to create magnificent displays which immediately capture one's attention from the very beginning. I delight in sampling, and so can you, those very fruit which are all local and yet, rarely seen in the local retail market. The last fruit festival offered a delicious array of local fruit kebabs, absolutely juicy. Just one of the many fruity treats which await you. Here is the best place to test taste Trinidad's finest fruit. I cannot resist the delectable sugar apple and sweet nectar of the sapodilla. A fun fact for chocolate lovers: our local cocoa beans are internationally famous for their depth of flavour and high nutritional value, second only to those produced in Madagascar. Come see what treats our local experts have created from this rich cocoa source.

48. WATCH THE SUN SET AT BAGO'S BEACH BAR, TOBAGO

Big treats all in one: the sea, sand, sunsets and the bar. This authentic beach bar setting is far better than what you get at a resort, in my opinion. However, if you are staying at the Coco Reef Hotel this cool hotspot is just next door. You will be swayed to leave and join in on the fun just on the other side as locals' laughter at the bar beckons you to join the good fun. Oh, you will love it. Just a walk down from Pigeon

Point Road and you will arrive at the perfect spot where you can spend the entire afternoon sipping fairly priced margaritas, piña coladas and just about anything. Though it's more of a bar than a fancy restaurant they do serve up some good burgers, fish, crab and dumpling and shrimp roti respectively. The owners and staff are great folks and good fun. Stay till six o'clock for a beautiful romantic sunset. Show off your skills on Saturday, their karaoke night. Overall, you will be happy to have stopped here.

49. ESCAPE THE CROWD – HIGHLAND WATERFALL, TOBAGO

How would you like to visit the highest single drop waterfall in Tobago? Just a cool trek through the lush green forest and across the river and you are there. If you book this awesome tour with Destination Trinidad and Tobago, every important aspect of preparation for this journey will be well taken care of for you. No worries! Pick up from and drop off to your hotel in Scarborough or Crown Point and environs is provided at no extra charge. Also, light refreshments are provided and all entrance fees are covered. Furthermore, with certified tour guides your safety comes first. Rest assured this could be your best adventure yet: a scenic drive across the island to the village of Les Coteaux will soon lead you to this seldom visited and well preserved natural oasis. Dress very comfortably, choose closed shoes, pack your swimming trunks and ready your nerves as you dare to dive into the deep plunge pool between the steep and rocky walls of the gorge. Or you can just relax comfortably in the surrounding area. Either way, this trip is ideal for families with children five years and over and requires a minimum of two persons per group. The tour begins around mid-morning, lasts roughly five hours and is packed with activity so I say it is well worth the money.

50. "LIME" BY SHARK RIVER

Take nothing but pictures leave nothing but footprints, kill nothing but time, says the welcome sign at Matura's Environmentally Sensitive Area, Shark River. Tucked into Northern Range between the villages of Matelot and Grand Riviere this sheltered spot makes a perfect getaway for all, including the wildlife that forage there. Bring a camera as you may spot deer, ocelots, porcupines, howler monkeys and even the critically-endangered pawi. You can look them up online before coming so you know what they look like. I suppose you have been wondering why it's called Shark River. Several years ago, the high tide would cause a swash of sea water into the river's mouth bringing with it a plethora of marine life including baby sharks which wandered upstream. Fear not because this no longer occurs as the river is but a shadow of its former self, not as wide or open but still loads of fun. With a number of shallow spots for wading and a few spots just deep enough for swimming, this makes a perfect destination for kids and adults alike. Bring a bath suit. The more adventurous among you can safely venture upstream where you will delight in the geographical structures there: gorges, waterfalls and tiny plunge pools.

TOP REASONS TO BOOK THIS TRIP

Natural Landscape: A stunningly wide variety of natural beauty.

Cuisine: Culturally innovative, spicy sweet and savoury dishes.

"Liming:" Happy culture of celebrating everything with a "lime."

Jamilah Beatrice

Bonus Book

50 THINGS TO KNOW ABOUT PACKING LIGHT FOR TRAVEL

Pack the Right Way Every Time

Author: Manidipa Bhattacharyya

Jamilah Beatrice

Edited by Melanie Howthorne

Introduction

He who would travel happily
must travel light.

-Antoine de Saint-Exupéry

Travel takes you to different places from seas and mountains to deserts and much more. In your travels you get to interact with different people and their cultures. You will, however, enjoy the sights and interact positively with these new people even more, if you are travelling light.

When you travel light your mind can be free from worry about your belongings. You do not have to spend precious vacation time waiting for your luggage to arrive after a long flight. There is be no chance of your bags going missing and the best part is that you need not pay a fee for checked baggage.

People who have mastered this art of packing light will root for you to take only one carry-on, wherever you go. However, many people can find it really hard to pack light. More so if you are travelling with children. Differentiating between "must have" and "just in case" items is the starting point. There will be ample shopping avenues at your destination which are just waiting to be explored.

Jamilah Beatrice

This book will show you 'packing' in a new 'light' –
pun intended – and help you to embrace light
packing practices for all of your future travels.

Off to packing!

Dedication

I dedicate this book to all the travel buffs that I know,
who have given me great insights into the contents of
their backpacks.

About The Author

Manidipa Bhattacharyya is a creative writer and editor, with an education in English literature and Linguistics. After working in the IT industry for seven long years she decided to call it quits and follow her heart instead. Manidipa has been ghost writing, editing, proof reading and doing secondary research services for many story tellers and article writers for about three years. She stays in Kolkata, India with her husband and a busy two year old. In her own time Manidipa enjoys travelling, photography and writing flash fiction.

Manidipa believes in travelling light and never carries anything that she couldn't haul herself on a trip. However, travelling with her child changed the scenario. She seemed to carry the entire world with her for the baby on the first two trips. But good sense prevailed and she is again working her way to becoming a light traveler, this time with a kid.

Jamilah Beatrice

The Right Travel Gear

1. Choose Your Travel Gear Carefully

While selecting your travel gear, pick items that are light weight, durable and most importantly, easy to carry. There are cases with wheels so you can drag them along – these are usually on the heavy side because of the trolley. Alternatively a backpack that you can carry comfortably on your back, or even a duffel bag that you can carry easily by hand or sling across your body are also great options. Whatever you choose, one thing to keep in mind is that the luggage itself should not weigh a ton, this will give you the flexibility to bring along one extra pair of shoes if you so desire.

2. Carry The Minimum Number Of Bags

Selecting light weight luggage is not everything. You need to restrict the number of bags you carry as well. One carry-on size bag is ideal for light travel. Most carriers allow one cabin baggage plus one purse, handbag or camera bag as long as it slides under the seat in front. So technically, you can carry two items of luggage without checking them in.

3. Pack One Extra Bag

Always pack one extra empty bag along with your essential items. This could be a very light weight duffel bag or even a sturdy tote bag which takes up minimal space. In the event that you end up buying a lot of souvenirs, you already have a handy bag to stuff all that into and do not have to spend time hunting for an appropriate bag.

I'm very strict with my packing and have everything in its right place. I never change a rule. I hardly use anything in the hotel room. I wheel my own wardrobe in and that's it.

Charlie Watts

Clothes & Accessories

4. Plan Ahead

Figure out in advance what you plan to do on your trip. That will help you to pick that one dress you need for the occasion. If you are going to attend a wedding then you have to carry formal wear. If not, you can ditch the gown for something lighter that will be comfortable during long walks or on the beach.

5. Wear That Jacket

Remember that wearing items will not add extra luggage for your air travel. So wear that bulky jacket that you plan to carry for your trip. This saves space and can also help keep you warm during the chilly flight.

6. Mix and Match

Carry clothes that can be interchangeably used to reinvent your look. Find one top that goes well with a couple of pairs of pants or skirts. Use tops, shirts and jackets wisely along with other accessories like a scarf or a stole to create a new look.

7. Choose Your Fabric Wisely

Stuffing clothes in cramped bags definitely takes its toll which results in wrinkles. It is best to carry wrinkle free, synthetic clothes or merino tops. This will eliminate the need for that small iron you usually bring along.

8. Ditch Clothes Pack Underwear

Pack more underwear and socks. These are the things that will give you a fresh feel even if you do not get a chance to wear fresh clothes. Moreover these are easy to wash and can be dried inside the hotel room itself.

9. Choose Dark Over Light

While picking your clothes choose dark coloured ones. They are easy to colour coordinate and can last longer before needing a wash. Accidental food spills and dirt from the road are less visible on darker clothes.

10. Wear Your Jeans

Take only one pair of Jeans with you, which you should wear on the flight. Remember to pick a pair that can be worn for sightseeing trips and is equally eloquent for dinner. You can add variety by adding light weight cargoes and chinos.

11. Carry Smart Accessories

The right accessory can give you a fresh look even with the same old dress. An intelligent neck-piece, a couple of bright scarves, stoles or a sarong can be used in a number of ways to add variety to your clothing. These light weight beauties can double up as a nursing cover, a light blanket, beach wear, a modesty cover for visiting places of worship, and also makes for an enthralling game of peek-a-boo.

12. Learn To Fold Your Garments

Seasoned travellers all swear by rolling their clothes for compact and wrinkle free packing. Bundle packing, where you roll the clothes around a central object as if tying it up, is also a popular method of compact and wrinkle free packing. Stacking folded clothes one on top of another is a big no-no as it makes creases extreme and they are difficult to get rid of without ironing.

13. Wash Your Dirty Laundry

One of the ways to avoid carrying loads of clothes is to wash the clothes you carry. At some places you might get to use the laundry services or a Laundromat but if you are in a pinch, best solution is to wash them yourself. If that is the plan then carrying quick drying clothes is highly recommended, which most often also happen to be the wrinkle free variety.

14. Leave Those Towels Behind

Regular towels take up a lot of space, are heavy and take ages to dry out. If you are staying at hotels they will provide you with towels anyway. If you are travelling to a remote place, where the availability of towels look doubtful, carry a light weight travel towel of viscose material to do the job.

15. Use A Compression Bag

Compression bags are getting lots of recommendation now days from regular travellers. These are useful for saving space in your luggage when you have to pack bulky dresses. While packing for the return trip, get help from the hotel staff to arrange a vacuum cleaner.

Footwear

16. Put On Your Hiking Boots

If you have plans to go hiking or trekking during your trip, you will need those bulky hiking boots. The best way to carry them is to wear them on flight to save space and luggage weight. You can remove the boots once inside and be comfortable in your socks.

17. Picking The Right Shoes

Shoes are often the bulkiest items, along with being the dainty if you are a female. They need care and take up a lot of space in your luggage. It is advisable therefore to pick shoes very carefully. If you plan to do a lot of walking and site seeing, then wearing a pair of comfortable walking shoes are a must. For more formal occasions you can carry durable, light weight flats which will not take up much space.

18. Stuff Shoes

If you happen to pack a pair of shoes, ensure you utilize their hollow insides. Tuck small items like rolled up socks or belts to save space. They will also be easy to find.

Toiletries
19. Stashing Toiletries

Carry only absolute necessities. Airline rules dictate that for one carry-on bag, liquids and gels must be in 3.4 ounce (100ml) bottles or less, and must be packed in a one quart zip-lock bag. If you are planning to stay in a hotel, the basic things will be provided for you. It's best is to buy the rest from the local market at your destination.

20. Take Along Tampons

Tampons are a hard to find item in a lot of countries. Figure out how many you need and pack accordingly. For longer stays you can buy them online and have them delivered to where you are staying.

21. Get Pampered Before You Travel

Some avid travellers suggest getting a pedicure and manicure just the day before travelling. This not only gives you a well kept look, you also save the trouble of packing nail polish. Remember, every little bit of weight reduced adds up.

Electronics
22. Lugging Along Electronics

Electronics have a large role to play in our lives today. Most of us cannot imagine our lives away from our phones, laptops or tablets. However while travelling, one must consider the amount of weight these electronics add to our luggage. Thankfully smart phones come along with all the essentials tools like a camera, email access, picture editing tools and more. They are smart to the point of eliminating the need to carry multiple gadgets. Choose a smart phone that suits all your requirements and travel with the world in your palms or pocket.

23. Reduce the Number of Chargers

If you do travel with multiple electronic devices, you will have to bear the additional burden of carrying all their chargers too. Check if a single charger can be used for multiple devices. You might also consider investing in a pocket charger. These small devices support multiple devices while keeping you charged on the go.

24. Travel Friendly Apps

Along with smart phones come numerous apps, which are immensely helpful in our travels. You name it and you have an app for it at hand – take pictures, sharing with friends and family, torch to light dark roads, maps, checking flight/train times, find hotels and many other things. Use these smart alternatives to traditional items like books to eliminate weight and save space.

I get ideas about what's essential when packing my suitcase.

-Diane von Furstenberg

Travelling With Kids

25. Bring Along the Stroller

Kids might enjoy walking for a while but they soon tire out and a stroller is the just the right thing for them to rest in while you continue your tour. Strollers also double duty as a luggage carrier and shopping bag holder. Remember to pick a light weight, easy to handle brand of stroller. Better yet, find out in advance if you can rent a stroller at your destination.

26. Bring Only Enough Diapers for Your Trip

Diapers take up a lot of space and add to the weight of your luggage. Therefore it is advisable to carry just enough diapers to last through the trip and a few for afterwards, till you buy fresh stock at your destination. Unless of course you are travelling to a really remote area, in which case you have no choice but to carry the load. Otherwise diapers are something you will find pretty easily.

27. Take Only A Couple Of Toys

Children are easily attracted by new things in their environment. While travelling they will find numerous 'new' objects to scrutinize and play with. Packing just one favorite toy is enough, or if there is no favorite toy leave out all of them in favor of stories or imaginary games.

28. Carry Kid Friendly Snacks

Create a small snack counter in your bag to store away quick bites for those sudden hunger pangs. Depending on the child's age this could include chocolates, raisins, dry fruits, granola bars or biscuits. Also keep a bottle of water handy for your little one. These things do not add much weight and can be adjusted in a handbag or knapsack.

29. Games to Carry

Create some travel specific, imaginary games if you have slightly grown up children, like spot the attractions. Keep a coloring book and colors handy for in-flight or hotel time. Apps on your smart phone can keep the children engaged with cartoons and story books. Older children are often entertained by games available on phones or tablets. This cuts the weight of luggage down while keeping the kids entertained.

30. Let the Kids Carry Their Load

A good thing is to start early sharing of responsibilities. Let your child pick a bag of his or her choice and pack it themselves. Keep tabs on what they are stuffing in their bags by asking if they will be using that item on the trip. It could start out being just an entertainment bag initially but with growing years they will learn to sort the useful from the superfluous. Children as little as four can maneuver a small trolley suitcase like a pro- their experience in pull along toys credit. If you are worried that you may be pulling it for them, you may want to start with a backpack.

31. Decide on Location for Children to Sleep

While on a trip you might not always get a crib at your destination, and carrying one will make life all the more difficult. Instead call ahead to see if there are any cribs or roll out beds for children. You may even put blankets on the floor. Weave them a story about camping and they will gladly sleep without any trouble.

32. Get Baby Products Delivered At Your Destination

If you are absolutely paranoid about not getting your favourite variety of diaper or brand of baby food, check out online stores like amazon.com for services in your destination city. You can buy things online ahead of your travel and get them delivered to your hotel upon arrival.

33. Feeding Needs Of Your Infants

If you are travelling with a breastfed infant, you save the trouble of carrying bottles and bottle sanitization kits. For special food, or medications, you may need to call ahead to make sure you have a refrigerator where you are staying.

34. Feeding Needs of Your Toddler

With the progression from infancy to toddler, their dietary requirements too evolve. You will have to pack some snacks for travelling time. Fresh fruits and vegetables can be purchased at your destination. Most of the cities you travel to in whichever part of the world, will have baby food products and formulas, available at the local drug-store or the supermarket.

35. Picking Clothes for Your Baby

Contrary to popular belief, babies can do without many changes of clothes. At the most pack 2 outfits per day. Pack mix and match type clothes for your little one as well. Pick things which are comfortable to wear and quick to dry.

36. Selecting Shoes for Your Baby

Like outfits, kids can make do with two pairs of comfortable shoes. If you can get some water resistant shoes it will be best. To expedite drying wet shoes, you can stuff newspaper in them then wrap them with newspaper and leave them to dry overnight.

37. Keep One Change of Clothes Handy

Travelling with kids can be tricky. Keep a change of clothes for the kids and mum handy in your purse or tote bag. This takes a bit of space in your hand luggage but comes extremely handy in case there are any accidents or spills.

38. Leave Behind Baby Accessories

Baby accessories like their bed, bath tub, car seat, crib etc. should be left at home. Many hotels provide a crib on request, while car seats can be borrowed from friends or rented. Babies can be given a bath in the hotel sink or even in the adult bath tub with a little bit of water. If you bring a few bath toys, they can be used in the bath, pool, and out of water. They can also be sanitized easily in the sink.

39. Carry a Small Load Of Plastic Bags

With children around there are chances of a number of soiled clothes and diapers. These plastic bags help to sort the dirt from the clean inside your big bag. These are very light weight and come in handy to other carry stuff as well at times.

Pack with a Purpose

40. Packing for Business Trips

One neutral-colored suit should suffice. It can be paired with different shirts, ties and accessories for different occasions. One pair of black suit pants could be worn with a matching jacket for the office or with a snazzy top for dinner.

41. Packing for A Cruise

Most cruises have formal dinners, and that formal dress usually takes up a lot of space. However you might find a tuxedo to rent. For women, a short black dress with multiple accessory options will do the trick.

42. Packing for A Long Trip Over Different Climates

The secret packing mantra for travel over multiple climates is layering. Layering traps air around your body creating insulation against the cold. The same light t-shirt that is comfortable in a warmer climate can be the innermost layer in a colder climate.

Reduce Some More Weight

43. Leave Precious Things At Home

Things that you would hate to lose or get damaged leave them at home. Precious jewelry, expensive gadgets or dresses, could be anything. You will not require these on your trip. Leave them at home and spare the load on your mind.

44. Send Souvenirs by Mail

If you have spent all your money on purchasing souvenirs, carrying them back in the same bag that you brought along would be difficult. Either pack everything in another bag and check it in the airport or get everything shipped to your home. Use an international carrier for a secure transit, but this could be more expensive than the checking fees at the airport.

45. Avoid Carrying Books

Books equal to weight. There are many reading apps which you can download on your smart phone or tab. Plus there are gadgets like Kindle and Nook that are thinner and lighter alternatives to your regular book.

Check, Get, Set, Check Again

46. Strategize Before Packing

Create a travel list and prepare all that you think you need to carry along. Keep everything on your bed or floor before packing and then think through once again – do I really need that? Any item that meets this question can be avoided. Remove whatever you don't really need and pack the rest.

47. Test Your Luggage

Once you have fully packed for the trip take a test trip with your luggage. Take your bags and go to town for window shopping for an hour. If you enjoy your hour long trip it is good to go, if not, go home and reduce the load some more. Repeat this test till you hit the right weight.

48. Add a Roll Of Duct Tape

You might wonder why, when this book has been talking about reducing stuff, we're suddenly asking you to pack something totally unusual. This is because when you have limited supplies, duct tape is immensely helpful for small repairs – a broken bag, leaking zip-lock bag, broken sunglasses, you name it and duct tape can fix it, temporarily.

49. List of Essential Items

Even though the emphasis is on packing light, there are things which have to be carried for any trip. Here is our list of essentials:

• Passport/Visa or any other ID

- Any other paper work that might be required on a trip like permits, hotel reservation confirmations etc.

- Medicines – all your prescription medicines and emergency kit, especially if you are travelling with children

- Medical or vaccination records

- Money in foreign currency if travelling to a different country

- Tickets- Email or Message them to your phone

50. Make the Most of Your Trip

Wherever you are going, whatever you hope to do we encourage you to embrace it whole-heartedly. Take in the scenery, the culture and above all, enjoy your time away from home.

On a long journey even a straw weighs heavy.

-Spanish Proverb

Packing and Planning Tips

A Week before Leaving

- Arrange for someone to take care of pets and water plants

- •Stop mail and newspaper

- Notify Credit Card companies where you are going.

- Change your thermostat settings

- Car inspected, oil is changed, and tires have the correct pressure.

- Passports and id is up to date.

- Pay bills.

- Copy important items and download travel Apps.

- Start collecting small bills for tips

Right Before Leaving

- Clean out refrigerator.

- Empty garbage cans.

- Lock windows.

- Make sure you have the right ID with you.

- Bring cash for tips.

- Remember travel documents.

- Lock door behind you.

- Remember wallet.

- Unplug items in house and pack chargers.

Jamilah Beatrice

Read other Greater Than a Tourist Books

Jamilah Beatrice

> TOURIST

Visit Greater Than a Tourist for Free Travel Tips
http://GreaterThanATourist.com

Sign up for the Greater Than a Tourist Newsletter for discount days, new books, and travel information:
http://eepurl.com/cxspyf

Follow us on Facebook for tips, images, and ideas:
https://www.facebook.com/GreaterThanATourist

Follow us on Pinterest for travel tips and ideas:
http://pinterest.com/GreaterThanATourist

Follow us on Instagram for beautiful travel images:
http://Instagram.com/GreaterThanATourist

Jamilah Beatrice

> TOURIST

Please leave your honest review of this book on Amazon and Goodreads. Please send your feedback to GreaterThanaTourist@gmail.com as we continue to improve the series. Thank you. We appreciate your positive and constructive feedback. Thank you.

Jamilah Beatrice

NOTES

Printed in Great
Britain
by Amazon